H.I.T.O.P.S.

H.I.T.O.P.S.

Healing in Trauma Ownership, Prosperity, &

Self-Reflection

E. MORTAL

ISBN-13: 979-8-8692-7931-6

Icon Global Publishing
www.iconglobalpublishing.com

Printed in the United States of America

Foreword

Eric Wiley (aka E. Mortal) is a poet who I refer to as Lazarus, who like a Phoenix in poetry and life found himself rising up from the ashes. Putting his life in spoken word, allowing art to be a reflection of his life.

Eric is a man who has endured the downward spirals of tribulations and then fought through the trenches of trauma and pain to find his peace again. In this anthology of poems you will read the soul and heart of a man who made the decision to be a living poetic expression.

In this book "H.i.T.O.P.S.
(Healing in Trauma Ownership
Prosperity & Self-Reflection)",
you're about to embark on the bold
truth of healing, toxicity, growth
and self-discovery.
You will get lost in the journey of
a man losing love in more ways than
one while viewing the vulnerability
of a man in rare form as he
navigates through the rebuilding
process of his existence.

Lastly, he is a friend and brother
that I am grateful to know exists.
His character exemplifies the
definition of brotherhood.
Integrity, protector, comedian,
but most importantly a supportive

friend are only a few traits that highlight the makings of this man.

Readers and supporters, I present to you the author and proprietor of H.I.T.O.P.S. My brother and friend, Mr. Eric Wiley

Nate Graham Sr.

Acknowledgments

So here we are at the culmination of this endeavor. The space where I extend thanks and appreciation for the support that made this collection of poetry possible. This book is the product of a lengthy healing process that began much later than it should but occurred right on time. During that process I received endless support from key people in my life and I want their names and contributions to live on this page as they live in my heart. Mom, I named the font after you (Shiree) because making you a part of this is so important to me. Your transition has prevented your physical presence in so many important milestones so being able to write you into this means the world to me. Anika, this book would not exist without the us we were or the healing we both needed in our lives. Thank you for all that you are and for helping me create two of the most important people in my life. Tee, you have been ten toes down since we met in Stuttgart good brother. I love you and appreciate your generous spirit and your friendship. Shannon, my appreciation for all that you are and have been means more to me than I say but your love, support, and encouragement has helped me become a version of myself that is no longer handicapped by the

overwhelming desire to seek
permission from others to be
myself.

Sister Ismail, thank you for
pouring your creative genius into
this book cover and for the
countless gestures of kindness you
have extended to me as a fellow
creative.

To the Clubhouse Poetry
community, I extend my
gratitude for being an
environment that cultivated
growth and consistency in my
poetry. I love you for being the
family of creatives I needed
during a challenging quarantine
period for the world. I extend a

special thanks to the incomparable Stina Jone' for your love, support, encouragement, and perspective without fail during my moments of need. To the Oliver's, your unconditional love and support in my life has been nothing short of a blessing. The energy you all poured into me personally and professionally means the world to me. Nate, you have become my beloved brother and creative soul mate as we often find ourselves on the same wavelength completing each other's thoughts while striving to gain additional mastery in the most underrated high art form called poetry. I am thankful for our frequent conversations and your ability to match energy in friendship, fatherhood, and servant leadership! Btw, eff you, 101! Poetry Lounge Houston, I thank you for being the catalyst to spark my desire to become a spoken word artist and for being my poetry home for over twenty years!

Lastly, I would like to thank my father, Frank Wiley, as you checked on me frequently to make sure I was doing well as I faced hardship and still moving forward. Dad, your counsel, patience, encouragement, humor, and wisdom saturated perspective has always been vital to my growth, and I

love you for always striving to
give me the best of you.

Dedication

For anyone that ever believed they needed permission from the world when they only really needed permission from themselves. You were born on purpose, now find greatness in it too!

CHAPTER 1: Healing in Trauma

Losing my Grip

Excuse these trauma bars, please

Born from moments of bondage that tried to devour me

I was caught in a vortex of finger pointing and lack of accountability

Compromising the dexterity of my grip on sanity

This trauma tainted energy was poisoning my headspace with negativity

Trying to snatch me back to that sunken place

where depression reigns supreme

But I peeped the scene that echoed remnants

of nightmares that were once my daily routine

Then I reached out and found out

I got an all-star team

willing to go to bat for me

Got some guidance that allowed me to focus on things relevant to me

Those elements led me down a path of healing

But this thing ain't all peaches and cream

Don't get it twisted cause you might miss the gist of it

I'm having more fun now

But the work ain't quite done now

Everyday I battle moments of rage from a dark place

Where that "I wish a motherfucker would" part of me stays

Because I'm one bad decision from making black history in the worst way

So I stay on my warrior in the garden shit

My pen became a catalyst of balance and zen

When I tweaked it with the proper dose
of discipline

I got one hand to pen these trauma bars
while the other holds tight to reality

Cause this is a season of essentials and
ain't no taking L's for me

Just lessons on this journey towards a
prosperous poet

that will always remember the
traumatized me

While I go toe to toe with an invisible foe

just so I can give my sons the best of me

Removing the collage of drama

On display in the foyer of my mentality

I'm cleaning house now

Cancelling replays of doubt now

So that

I'm better equipped to flourish you see

No longer waiting for others to nourish
me

I don't need them to wipe me down

I got the tools now

Did some shadow work and walked in the
light to sage this vessel down

cause I'm on purpose now

My mantra is manifesting the healing me

Guiding me through Aset

As I set boundaries and manage the
type of energy I allow around me

I be the architect of positivity
permeating my reality with the richness
of relief

My grip may slip but I won't lose touch
of the best parts born of me

Stepping away from the place of
compromised morality

A prime element of self-care
replenishing my mortality

Edifying these malnourished pieces of
me

Because

I'm done living in the shadows of someone
else's

Dark twisted fantasy

The Breaking of my Bones

I am a Witcher

Transformed by chaos and showered in contempt

By those whose belief in the powers that be

Allow empty words to overshadow what their eyes feel and their soul sees

A child of arrested development and accelerated growth

The demise of innocent eyes have me

Seeing the world through a lens of burnt orange resentment

The riverbanks of these sorrowful eyes
overflow as winds of self-indulgence
steal my focus

So, I open my third eye and close the
receptors that hinder my healing

Hoping to make a home where emotion and
logic can roam

On the other side of this breaking of my
bones

Animosity kicks like a vengeful bitch!

And silence is interrupted by the crack
of a fracture

Revealing the treasure soul suckers
chase after

My marrow is the gift that comes from
the hollow

The scent of success is a promise of
sustenance these zombies of mediocrity
follow

Carnivorous dreams of gnashing teeth

Tearing the cloak of my insecurities like
flesh

Fear, doubt, and the pressure of
stress pour from veins

A steady flow as it seeps, a constant
drip when it leaks.

They want to ingest me while I breathe

Mental stability is the victim of
kidnapping

No ransom requested

Tortured like a chattel slave

My peace has been tarred, feathered,
and set ablaze for entertainment on
Sundays

While at war with the scent of fear that
strangles the air I inhale

I can smell the promise of purpose in a
forest of ignorant confused souls

Its lavender notes are lined with scents
of jasmine that pull me along this

Underground Railroad to liberation

Transfixed

on the NorthStar lit with ancestors'
remnants

While trying not to fail myself

This discontent spirit yearns for calm

But I must first wash away the
obscurity of detachment

Clothe myself in the wardrobe of
intention

These shoes of discomfort are my
barometer

For this breaking of my bones

Multiple contusions

Black and blue bruises

Become the currency of this transaction

Bones bent at angles that make no sense
beyond the screams wrenched from the
voice box of my feelings

It's a push and pull struggle

Trying to escape a cage I didn't know existed

The warning signs of this dead-end road must have been written in another language

Lack of awareness dims the light of hope holding me in anguish

While failures seductress flirts with me

I must be hallucinating because this can't be a dream

It's a nightmare fueled by fear

That this sphere I hold my nakedness in

Will become a graveyard for the feelings within

As I die to this breaking of my bones

I'm OK

You may hear a common phrase like: I'm ok

Sometimes it's prudent to investigate
this common phrase in a loving way

Because that turn of phrase is often
tied to tumultuous days and dark
thoughts

Tangled up into unsolved problems have
me feeling lost

I never talked about this but it needs to
be said

To alleviate the stress of holding this
burden in my anxiety riddled head

I carry the stress of failure in my
heart

It aches with the force of blows from a
sledgehammer

You can feel the lumps thump from the
impact that pushes against my solo
plexus

Until an explosion of trauma claws it way
into the light

Like a hostile alien incubated in the dark
parts of my soul

And I, a once naked canvas has been
splashed with the regret of bad
decisions

A horror story flashing across the
screen of my face

Disfigured by desperation, disbelief and
embarrassment

This contorted pain goes against the
grain of peace leaving a faded yellow
hue of vibrant hubris now lost

Exhausted and emptied into the greedy
vessel of other peoples vanity

Mixed against the faded gray road
paving its way to my anguish

Seeking a way to the other side of the
heartache held inside far too long

Negativity coalesced into a collective
that has become too strong to contain

It manifests in rage instead of being
purged in healing

Pulsating through my fingers

My body powers up to expel a lightning
strike of destruction

into a mass of collateral damage with
beating hearts

I fight the habit to force it back down
and hold it in

My skin keloids in disapproval

worn from being used to store toxic
energy

The ink from my pen gives me a release

An electric blue sigh of relief cools the
caverns of concern

as howling winds of worry dissipate

Before the cold and warm fronts tussle
to re-up weather born drama

I am a tropical storm of compressed
emotions making landfall

On a collision course with the storm-
breaker that is my healin

Because I'm tired of avoiding a dungeon
of imprisoned feelings

At the end of the day, when my
disposition is in conflict with a common
phrase most men mention

I'm really going through and I don't
know how to breakthrough this hidden pain

So let me be the one to say

I'm not ok

At Odds

The words that leave your lips burden
my heart with pain

You speak with an ugliness that drips
disdain

A sharp tongue untamed can cut deep

Leaving bittersweet memories

Images of a time when I became We

You used to be an inspiration to me

But these days you prefer to be enemies

No matter my effort to maintain peace

You prefer to provoke conflict

Before my military commitments create
distance

It seems a recurring theme to fight
before I leave

So, you can spend that time entertaining
and exploring other things

The frequency of these moments seem
well planned

Like you need to free up your time for
another man

If someone has your attention then do
your thing

Ain't no need for the fuckery and
dramatic scenes

If the grass over there is green and
gets the water flowing in your well
spring

Far be it from me to be a source of
misery

Just let me go and be free

Because honestly I would rather be alone
if the pictures I paint are selfish
scenes

Why torture your seed, yourself, or me?

There is no logic to your behavior

Pettiness is not an appealing flavor

You set us all up for failure when you
pick a fight in full view of our child

And taking part in that crushes my
heart

To see him scared leaves a scar

I was embarrassed at myself for
allowing you to pull me into that nonsense

Never again

I will leave before I repeat another one
of those moments

That put my son in jeopardy of being
broken

Going forward is my goal

No more days of letting frustration with
your faults become a stranglehold.

You can continue to sidestep and deny
your fault in these fights

You can call your ex-boyfriend about who
is wrong or right.

But I can save you the time

All you have to do is say the words and I
will oblige

But mark these words before you make a
decision that brings tears to your eyes

Keep in mind

I don't come back when I say goodbye

Do your worst, I'll move!

You can have the last word and the
finger pointing too

If it stops this roller coaster ride of
emotional harassment and verbal abuse

you trying to get me to ride with you

I just wanna end this over saturated
experience of one-way fulfillment

Where your needs had preferential
treatment while mine sat in a holding
pattern

because you didn't understand the
assignment

Apparently, the jokes on me

considering how consistently you
disregarded what mattered to me

No matter how plainly I'd speak

the clues I'd leave

the absence of subtlety

when I verbalized my needs repetitively

Everything else became a priority

I poured into you but couldn't get you to
replenish me

Passion's kiss

Time to find pleasure in the warmth
between your thighs

Therapy to seal the idiosyncrasies that
created gaps in our marital seams

So we could float into happily ever after

These were simple things I asked of you

Now you're on an emotional tirade trying
to make misery a regular component of
my days

Because you can't rationalize that what
I did for me was not about you

Getting my needs met became an
undeniable pull to retain my sanity

But in your mind it's all about
accountability when the microscope of
judgment skips you and lands on me

Well, here's the part that is still too
difficult for you to process

I was drowning and you wouldn't even
throw me a lifeline

Yea I did some fucked up shit that
fractured you

It was designed to edify me, but it
carried a byproduct of pain for you when
I decided I

would no longer hide my infidelity and be
straight up with you

Now you've retreated to a place where
you can't hear shit I say but you want me
to listen to you

And as I speak to both of our truths

it's become clear that this is who you've
always been and what you always do

So, I yield

Do your worst, I'll move!

You can have the last word and the house
too

Just leave me the fuck alone and work on
healing that pettiness you still carry
with you

The Unexpected

We had an ugly ending born of a
beautiful beginning that was once soaked
in love

But when fools rush in tragedy can
strike with the suddenness of lightning

And I can't help but consider the things
we missed as we made quick feet down
the road to bliss

Until we lost track of what made this
impossible task seem so right

Ending up on a path that would
eventually have me shaking my head at
the red flags waving at me in hindsight

I remember

The way this decade of togetherness
started before unchecked warfare made
us spiritually departed

We came straight out of a fairytale

Black love destined to prevail

Highlights flooding timelines all across
Facebook of the leaps and bounds we took

Courting you from another continent with
conviction because I just knew this was
what God intended

But maybe I missed the message that
said this is only a test

Colorblind to the warning signs that
screamed

Don't give it your best because she not
quite ready yet

and neither are you for that matter

But I didn't listen because my unmended
heart wanted a win more than it needed
to purge traces of poison still flowing
through my veins

So once again I'm dancing a slow dance
with heartache only this time I got more
skin in the game

Fast forward to the here and now where
I'm still a facilitator of the wow factor
in your days

And yet the pride that used to
accompany this fact is redressed in a
new truth

that now the most recent wow I carved
across your heart left an impression in
the worst way

And it really ain't much I can say in my own defense

when I turned our world upside down on some Jerry Springer type ish

Reminders of my infidelity have me riding up and down on a seesaw of shame and rage wondering which side will win

The man of honor I once was, listed as MIA

Leaving a debt to be paid in resentment and heartache

Until seventy-seven minutes unlocked a path to forgiveness

Causin the trajectory of this journey to change

as we came to terms with the mistakes we
made

Talking through the breakdowns in our
communication

gave us both a chance to breathe again

But then

After I wiped the salty remnant of
tears and freed my upper lip from the
stench of my own self centeredness

I could smell the aroma of healing my
words carried to your ears

As tears of relief flowed to mend our
battered hearts of wounds inflicted

Hope stopped loving me from a distance
and took me by the hand

After my humility proved me worthy

So I thank you for the hearing, healing
and understanding both given and
received

Because now I feel reconnected to the
parts of me I've mourned for five
hundred and forty-seven days

There is no lesson more profound than one
that is unexpected

Because before I got the message

you could have

Crowned me King of the damned for
leaning to my own understanding

Aggrieved

Forgive my verbal wobble as I
emotionally waddle with swollen ankles
and lower back pain

Ready to birth a child of unspoken words
carrying names of all the trauma

toxic communication made

I dreamt of falling stars last night

So, I made a wish for a catalyst that
would let me express myself right

For a moment I wanted to recant it but
the thought vanished

Because I was quickly granted a gift of
ears that would hear all the things I
need to say

Needless to say, they weren't attached
to your heart or mind and that had me
feeling some type of way

So, I wrote my pain on a paperless page
after I knelt to pray

sat to meditate

I was guided to let the healing me speak
while sharing observations I've made

Because what good is a confession if it
hangs from a link of chains that have a
lockdown on change

Once upon a time

We talked about bearing witness to
relationship dynamics in our family
bloodlines and recognized some universal
truths

But we couldn't break the generational
curses because you thought what I
wanted to do was change you

When all I wanted was to help you
cleanse the traumatic lens you continue
to view life through

I want to tell you my actions never
stopped saying I love you even when I
was upset with you

So it hurt me as you traumatized me by
denying me reciprocity in that regard

Because that said your love for me is
conditional and if that's your truth

the love I have in my heart ain't really
meant for you

I wish I would have experienced the toxic parts of you before I made a long term investment

Because the pros were overshadowed by cons that should have given me pause

Unbreakable habits that became Lego's that built an ending we agree was truly tragic

How you handled my vulnerability was a critical element worthy of an in-depth assessment

Because if I can't breakdown with the one that says she gone hold me down

I may as well walk out the door right now

And when you tried to kick me out when we should have been talking it out

I knew that getting you to hear what I
needed to say was gonna be a tall order
and you have a lite appetite for looking
at yourself

You called me your King but fought me
every step of the way

Because you wanted to have things your
way

Now you Queen in a castle without a King

Trying to make my legacy head of the
household at nine years olds

as if bearing your emotional weight is a
healthy way for him to grow

And I'm on the outside wit a heavy heart
and tearful eyes

Wanting to cry but standing by

ready to help my sons make sense of
what's gonna be a lifelong ride

CHAPTER 2:
Ownership

The Edge of Healing

I betrayed my pen

Because the idea of dealing with my

feelings

left me in a state of unreadiness

And the thought of being vulnerable

creates significant unpleasantness

Born from indictments of excessive

sensitivity

Levied by peers in the days of my youth

And while I wish I could curse them for

stealing the possibility of relief with

emotional release

Accountability forces me to reconcile the

decision to abandon what dreams may

have come

were made by me

A perspective I was forced to confront

when a seasonal friend

read between the lines of my poetry

Highlighting the missing link that often

separates the good from great

Respectfully, he encouraged me to delve

into that component and give myself

permission to create a safe space

And as I strive to overcome my stubborn

nature and the coziness of a comfort zone

I share this summation as a declaration

of my dedication to bathe in the muddy

murkiness of my feelings

Because if ever I am remembered for

my pen

I want the realness of my life to splash

blank pages and color them with my truth

Like the seven-year torture of watching

the strongest woman I've ever known

slowly fade from the rigors of MS

Coupled with early onset dementia and

schizophrenia

Until what was left died a lonely death in

the back of an ambulance

The unwelcome call that came and how it

destroyed a seemingly normal day

When my pain shattered voice shared the

news with my father

Who was so overcome with sorrow that he

had to pull over on the freeway to make

room for tears to flow

Even though he and my mother divorced

before I turned three years old

A testimony to the impact she had on the

lives she touched

I remember a depression laden fog that

hugged me with suicidal thoughts until

they became as familiar as a lover's

embrace

Fueled by feelings of failure that I

should have done more for her

In a time when the word 'more' had no

face but still held a place in the mirror

of my soul

Even now tears still fill my eyes nearly

two decades after her transition

Because thoughts of her make me relive

pain that should have long ago been

purged

So here I am standing center stage with

my sorrow

On the edge of healing trying to walk
through the door to something than
better than this
Fighting the urge to say fuck this
bullshit
Because pulling back the veil of what ails
me has thrown off my equilibrium
Turning the lies I tell myself upside
down like a bully shaking hurt from the
pockets of my soul
like currency
Truth be told
I'd rather be doing anything besides
feeling the way I am currently

Everything

Everything happens for a reason

Hardship has a season

And our palate doesn't always

welcome the flavor

Discomfort is rarely something to savor

when we have a taste for hope

Gluttony becomes a habit that's hard to

let go

When our eyes see more than

our stomach can hold

Even still

Don't waver from the commitment you
made in the beginning when things
seemed to be going your way

Don't negotiate with yourself because
you might come up short

You may lose focus entertaining the
retort that comes when things get tough

When your comfort zone whispers sweet
nothings that say where you are is enough

Complacency is a thief that steals focus
and leaves grief

Robbing you of opportunity to tune your
energy

Reach a harmonic frequency to secure a
future for the sake of legacy

It's a curious thing

How distraction tries to become the
ambassador to everything

This fate I made

Heart beating

Alarm beeping so I must be alive

Time to start this grind

I exhale and begin the routine

they say will lead to happiness, and a
plethora of other things

I brush my teeth in case some part of
this day

requires me to speak

Put the kettle on before washing my face

clean the slate of my existence

to make myself presentable for life

Fresh face shaven nice and tight

Hair combed and laid to the side

I think I got it right

Suit and tie swag with the matching messenger bag

on my way to get the success I'm meant to have

HURRY UP WAIT!

I almost forgot

I need my pill of perseverance to power up for the challenges I might face

I'm the Bill they trying to kill before I proceed to the next stage

So glad I got plenty for days to come or
the moment my walk becomes a run

I just gotta set the pace keep doing
what I'm doing and I'll win this race

I'm trying to get to the end so I begin

And when the curtain goes up I do it
again

This plight is meant to be simple like
black and white

But I get to see a little color

I keep it covered and ration it out
carefully

But

Each day fills wit more space

The gap between where I am and where
I wanna be has become great

But still, I feel the same

This was supposed to be different

Why doesn't my privilege kick in

Maybe I wasn't meant to benefit

The way I did it till the end

seemed the right way

All my work and this is the fate I made

I thought I was moving but I was still in
the same place because I ended up
spending my life the same way that I
spent my days

A Peek Inside

They peaked through a window and saw
heartbreak holding hands with disbelief

Talkin about how the foul smell of lies
clashed with the taste of memories
sautéed in serendipity

They conversed about how love held first
place as a favorite plate of soul food

Served on a porcelain dish garnished
with the hope of forever

Candied yams, macaroni and cheese, hot
water cornbread and collard greens, ox
tails, stuffing, and snap peas

Were sustenance born of need

Seasoned with salty caramel tears to
remind me that life can be bitter sweet

Sometimes we don't like the taste of fate
but when we gotta eat to survive being
picky doesn't always fit the need

So, we grin and bear it until our belly's
take their fill to pacify the hunger pains
of undelivered promises

Wooden floors creek from routines of love
as loved one's creep for a peek with
hungry eyes driven by a curious stomach

And slivers of light show the
refrigerated truth we keep cool so it
won't spoil before consumption

When no one is around and the thirst of
wanting makes us anxious for
companionship

We reach for water that will never fill
us because we don't know what to do with
our hands

Free

Of all the things I was told I could be

Free wasn't on the list that was
mentioned to me

They told me I could be anything I
wanted to be

But they didn't give me a blueprint they
just told me to do me

Cryptic comments masquerading as
guidance were nonsensical to me

They called me shy but said they saw
the greatness inside

Felt the power behind my attentive eyes

But they didn't know how to nurture my
growth

So I spent decades wondering how to
unlock the superpowers my soul holds

Until I became an alchemist and set my
own self free

I heard the secret and couldn't help but
believe it

Started speaking from a place of I Am
so I could finally be it

Now when they ask me who I am

A smile emerges as the response flows
freely

I'm a Guru of smithing words to be spoke
and heard

A maestro of weaving storylines using
subject predicate and verb

I'm an Essential Mortal poetically

a dope entity with big Taurus energy

I do dope shit

My flow froze the prose so I could poet

Into your chalice of understanding

This ain't rhetoric it's the light
illuminating your flight path so stick the
landing and get grounded in wisdom

Cultivated in experience

delivered by your favorite pewology
professor

Shots fired

At threats that must be addressed lest
your purpose expires

Process the presentation and don't fight
the urge to call me sire

After I seed your mind with supernova
fire

Bathed in the desire of the universe

Oludumare sent me the Orishas to keep
evil at bay

The ancestors speak to me in a variety
of ways and on good days

the message is clear

Understanding was the bridge that
brought me here

But sometimes my analytical mind is kicked into overdrive while I decipher the code

Simplify the complex and blend it with hope

Marinaded in faith

Step up and walk this way if you wanna get somewhere

The comfort zone you holding onto won't get you there

Because its teacher is using outdated information

You need this power blend of learn how to do you juice

It's a spiritual libation

Because the only thing keeping any of us

from truly being free is measured by

how we confine ourselves mentally

Nomadic Love

Love doesn't live here

But it visits frequently enough to tune
the vibrations of my frequency to truth

I find it in meals made from scratch by
these hands when I remember I am
enough

Love's bliss is a gentle kiss of energy
transfused by a muse

sending vibes that make my pen move

Love has become a good friend

that likes to hang with my kids

It ushers comfort in

when my oldest child smiles

It's got its own space that seems like a
favorite place in my second born's laugh

Love is a nomad walking its own path

I hear it in the songs I sing

Reminding me of beauty covered by
hardship's blemish

Trauma left scars but love delivered
healing

when peace came to me while meditating
under stars

Rescued by the exploits of a nomad by
heart

As love drifted my way guided by the
gods

I'm grateful it crossed paths with me
and was compelled to pause

Sometimes life makes it easy to forget

Love doesn't live here it just visits in
due season for unknown reasons

as an unexpected gift

And when I remembered love is its own
entity and not property to be owned

it became a regular addition to the
energy I invite into my home

The Lie

If we believe the lie

We spend a lifetime prioritizing elusive
things when what really matters is
family and the prosperity of peace

Admittedly

Invisible things can be hard to perceive
when doubt hangs its hat in your
headspace like uninvited guests with bad
table manners

Giving its two cents about the taste of a
meal never intended for their tastebuds

The ingredients you season your success
with doesn't fit their palate so they
leave bad reviews

Intended to discourage you like your
effort makes their bowels move

But the divine gave you an extraction
tool to discard the foundation of the
burden they try to build in you

Courage

This skeleton key you possess is an
umbrella of middle fingers meant to keep
you dry

when naysayers seek to rain pessimism on
your dreams

When the elites ask you to trade a
lifetime toiling fields for their stability
and the luxury of collecting material
things

Check it

You ever notice how our dreams are
subjected to abuse

Rewarded for the ability to do what's
expected for those that wanna life of
comfort at the expense of you

They buy your time to use and designate
pay at a deflated rate while you trade
decades until they use you up and
replace you with someone new the next
day

Intentionally neglected by our
willingness to conform to the status quo

We dim our light to the play the
background in someone's else's show

Introducing ourselves to the taste of
regret

But its full flavor is being prepared by the sacrifice of time we haven't surrendered yet

So the taste is a little bland

And this knowing makes me wonder how some make it through the world with their soul in one piece

But as I turned my observation towards my own area of development

I got a message in the mail from the supreme architect

He told me the ground I gave you build on is rough but it will yield plentiful crops

You just need to keep living water on hand to hydrate you on days when the

heat discourages you to plant the seeds
I have entrusted you

Find a way or make one to replenish
yourself with peace love and laughter

Cause when you're the author of your own
story there's no need to be afraid of the
next chapter

CHAPTER 3:
Prosperity

A Query for you

I abandoned distractions of capitalism for the truth of my pen

Put a pause on expecting gifts to be given

To dance wit this instrument for exploring tunes of life played for absorption

It be my accordion

Affording an auditory glimpse into the scope of my mental music notes

More often than not

I use it to cope

Carryin a bag of trauma covering
solutions to problems

That plague those wishing the world was
honest

Pockets of parables unfold like origami

Inside my mind when I spy the
juxtaposition of life

with this analytical gray matter linked
to observational eyes

Leaving me compelled to lift the veil of
infatuation binding sensations

that detract attention from the
colloquial code designed for destruction
by colonizers

I mixed a livener

for the punch-drunk masses moving like
they hungover

In an ironic twist of fate I moved away

from that vicious circle to create
cultivate and curate liberation

A focus intent on uniting a broken nation

Then I weaved a velvet-colored story
for storing hope and built a promontory
of analogies and metaphors to rise above
the wetness of a decadent atmosphere

Waging war against euphoria

The tip of my pen is an antagonist

to close minded foes in the folds of this
skin we live in

It seeks to deprive oppression the
oxygen being delivered to promote these
unnecessary splits

Blatantly given hate for the loner
lagging behind a school of fish

following a grouper blindly pursuing the
fate labeled a goal by raiders to the
onyx temple

of evolution

Corrupting the master plan of the first
ones to do it

as they sensed knowledge would manifest
a movement

when possessed by those that held the
truth of it in their DNA

We be subjected to time now

paying fines now

to finance the release of

A blueprint convoluted by layers of
allusion

hiding transcendental keys

I asked the ancestors to speak

with a gatekeeper on my behalf

Ogun sent the sharpness of his axe my
way

made my blade drip with the power of
blood orange ink

leading the charge to avenge souls of the
scavenged

By those that built an advantage so
gargantuan that takin from others has
become an physiological habit

Lastly, if you solved the riddle dwelling
in the middle

I got one final query to present you

Since the divine made me Essential, what
do you think He made you?

Alphabetical Poetical

A B C D

E - ternally the ambassador for the
source code you seek

I may be alphabetized at number five
but see seven to know the whole of me

And subtract one if you need to know
what you better NOT wit me

I hold the keys

To liberate thunder caught by lightning
trying to set your power free

Validate your desire to be and pollinate
your seeds with stardust from the
galaxy

I am wisdom

I'm not in position to share what I've
written

But I can share my thoughts if you'll
listen

Decipher the source code within the
ellipsis

Left by the gate keeper of the universe

Meant for one that can master the keys

to unlock doors holding the secrets we
seek

For instance

Deceit is the secret fake friends keep

My tired tongue speaks through raining
fire

Cutting away strings of torment

that belong to the puppet master of
purgatory

The blade I wield is mighty

and I was chosen to be its master

I traveled to Eden and lay prostrate
before the Griot's wet stone to sharpen
my words

Called home by the ancestors for
equipping

with tools made for ripping

The veils from truth seeking eyes

For those that go to the shadows to work
the residue of trauma left unchecked
inside

I salute you

Seeking to recruit you for service

Since your actions show the power of your
spirit

and the worth of it

Unconscious minds don't realize

Healing in trauma holds the prize

It hurts like hell but still good for your
health

The mental part swayed by the scars

left across your heart

It's just a matter of when you'll get
beyond twiddling your thumbs and move
past start

To the place rejuvenation was born

Reiki energy raking the weight of
negativity from souls once scorned

Energy transformed at the crossroads

of preparation and opportunity

Moving out of a fog of obscurity

Into purpose driven blessings exit right

Take a hard left into healing light

And set the cruise control for your
journey

to keep the vibrations of your energy
right

A Poet's Parable

I've been buried alive by a culture of
lies

that fear the truth of me

So they drape me in a casket of words
that siphon batteries

Making vessels too weak to sail in the
richness of truth

Polymaths of prosperity become
corrupted

converted into sentinels of disparity

Sparing me the joy of flowing freely

across a land that promised liberty

Strong arm tactics

to hinder every soul traveling this
dimension

in melanated vessels

I taste the bittersweet fruit grown
from seeds

We now know to be the original prejudice

Impeding progress

In the mediocrity of moments

highlighted by the hype of capitalistic
gain

But still, I move

Because I carry the perseverance to
solve riddles held hostage behind walls
of deception

The deceivers hold no shame and the
depth of this game makes the fallacy of
fame glow

like jewels meant to catch eyes

Pullin attention from crystals Mother
Earth designed

to regulate and rejuvenate natural vibes

It's a deceptively complex code

of fulfillment stealing nodes

that make light of passionate effort

tainted by the creators of this cinematic
shit show

Peep the scene sown by nightmares
dreamt on ocean floors by the nearly
forgotten

The preset of my DNA is wariness

an encoded warning from ancestors

that programmed my bloodline

Their generational connections created

A spiritual threat detection I can't
ignore

A survival mechanism designed to
identify murderers trying to kill the
ties that bind

I find my soul keeps time

with heartbeats of outrage

Beatin coral reefs like drums

Refusing to let us forget

that living water still takes up space

in dead lungs beneath the sea

Refusing to dilute ancestral respite

because vengeance doesn't have an
expiration date

Trauma transmutes into a tsunami of pain

riding waves of resistance

Seeking retribution from the
descendants of their captors

Because they tired (x2)

they say they tired

of waiting for us to reward their
sacrifice by drawing the blood of big
money legacies

still getting high off the hog that was
slaughtered to feed all of y'all

And all the smoke

born of greed's flame choke the dreams
of black folk in a controlled burn

Rudimentary tongs hold the precious
metal of unrefined souls

Impurities expelled until reflections of
reclamation mirror black Hebrew
Israelites

I am Them

I am Him

My adversaries see that I am grim

Rejectin false messages

Astral plane projectin

My third eye gaze penetrates

swaying shackled minds desperate to
find a cheat code to freedom until they
realize

that freedmen fight

Becomin the sacrifice tormented souls
need

Married to the pathway beginning that
next life

The only way to eternal life is carved in
this journey I walk in ritualistic
commitment

leaving a blueprint of footprints that
precede the mystery of finite moments

before I die

My battle cry is a call to kindred souls
listening trying to honor the investment
of my edifying existence

Burning Feet

I got nothing left but my burning feet

No fucks to give

Because my peace is too valuable

So please, if your energy is laced with foolishness

Stay the hell away from me

and I'll stay in my lane

Fuckery free

Protecting my peace is a prelude to maintaining my boundaries

as I heal and advocate for the child in me

My ID and EGO are now proud of me

When I walk by mirrors

I see them smiling at me

Cause I walked my ass right the fuck out
of that den of depression

Dead set on devouring me

A shift when I speak

Let's you feel the awakening of power in
me

Unchained

Breathing deep

Despite the fact I got nothing left but
these burning feet

The rest of me

Became a cautionary tale to a life lived
behind a veil of wanting permission

That was already given by the universe

The creator of a thousand galaxies
predestined my purpose before birth

To determine what I would be long
before my first breath

This plane of existence my test

Fail to try or try to bring out my best

Success that hangs with the weight of
chains on the necks of slaves

Liberation is imminent and I'm gonna get
it

By the edge of a blade, the heat of a
bullet, or the tip of my pen

Once these burning feet are gone

I pray my melanin draped soul will be
reborn again

Sounds of Silence

My silence sounds like

The manifestation of peace

vibrations of cool colored violet green

This space I'm in is a vibrant thing

Balance emanates from the stillness that
has joined this retreat

An impromptu extraction from
distractions and bad habits

Healing is my souls sustenance and I
gotta have it

A sublime ride of rejuvenation outside
the restrictions of time

It's the alchemy of a new vibe that's all
mine

And I wanna take a walk with it

Hold hands with this beautiful gift I
need to get into a relationship with

We can interlock fingers until the
newness of this sensation no longer feels
like puppy love

But I low key hope the energy never
fades

This self-love edification might be a
necessary element to my destination of
salvation

Sinning can be redeemed if you got
enough humility to bend a knee

Meditate and pray

Ask the ancestors to hold it down while
you work in the shadows

Seeking secrets beneath the shallows of
rhyme schemes

Discomfort is a key that liberates you
from the gallows of an unfulfilled life

wasted in the shade of contentment

Inspiration Exchange

It ain't no coincidence that I'm

articulate

Because the universe made me Griot for

the deliverance of wisdom

Gleaned from the knowledge of my

existence

I use imagination as a canvas

dripping the power of creative

presentations escaping pages with the

truth

of how our greatness was degraded

I've been tasked to give you the thing

that is seldom seen

These things

the creator weaved within are master
keys
for the win
I'm clutch when it comes to peeping the
imposters among us
Because discernment is among the gifts
that I radiate to bring about
change in a cold world
my range is limitless
and I'm living the uncertainty of a risk
laden life because my mic fights
the status quo of complacency like an
autistic savant unafraid of
martyrdom
I'm loc bae in a world of carbon copied
fades
My pen shaves the face of change close

If you like potent lines then snort this
dope
for high vibrations carrying the
calibration
to conquer the calamity
of a colonized mind demanding to be free
I ain't charging a fee on this one
because it goes beyond the distraction of
a divide diluted
The truth is
what I do mimics a period defined as
inter glacial
It's the divining line drawn from
A period of change
where the warmth of the climate is
indicative of the game I gave
at the outset of this inspiration exchange

My Lucky Pen

My lucky pen knows my needs

Tuning my vibes for writing is her area
of expertise

The physical touch she gives is a
language of love

breathing life into words

She knows her power and the magic we
can make when my energy creates
synergy with hers

She's a muse that moves my mood

when I'm trying to get through

Epiphanies be the source of alchemy

she likes to use

As a tool to excavate the aches taking up
space

in my heart

Her scythe cuts with irony as it sets
life free

liberating organs surrounded by dried
out veins

That attempted suicide

with self-deprecating thoughts

My pen pops severely

When my black boy joy needs to be
recharged

She knows her might in a fight

is deadlier than Excalibur

So don't come @ her

unless you want to see us both

And become victim to a legend in stories

yet to be told

We lethal in close quarters and deadly
from a distance

Weak pens go on sabbatical when we come
to visit

Bar for bar or fang and claw

words of our exploits drop jaws

Seventy ounces of awe is the norm

Our flow be liquid bear witness

like water we move with no form

You've been forewarned that coming for
us will leave you forlorn

My lucky pen be a place of zen

She's a healer helping me manage the
toxins

that accumulated within

as a threat to my wealth

A threat to my health

My pen knows my potential

she be training me

straining me

taking me into the depths of myself

My pen be a conduit for me

to cry, scream, or simply breathe

She spits out affirmations of my
humanity

whenever she be penning with me

She stay ten toes down around and around

We be merry if we stationary or walking
on clouds

of creativity

She don't miss
Told me she chose me cause she
that bitch
Ride or die no matter what it is because
she wit the shits

My pen knows I'm a force to be reckoned
with
because my vibe injects philosophical
highs for junkies of knowledge-based art

in need of a fix

My pen knows my mortality is an
essential

mix of the ingredients I be cooking
these poems wit
So I submit

It might be a good look for you to keep a
pen

you can write your way through this
thing called life with

Cause the benefits of it hits different
and I been walking in my power

ever since my pen whispered to me in the
witching hour

CHAPTER 4: Self-Reflection

How Vulnerable We Should Be

The heart is inherently wild and rarely tamed

For the song cry we each make has different words but tend to be the same

So our choice of expression is the only uniqueness that truly remains.

While trying to decipher the Morse code that is Life and what's in store,

We unknowingly make ourselves vulnerable to so much more

And the pain that precedes pleasure

evaporates with a smile,

causing joy, serenity and gratification

to linger awhile

The best of you and the best of me will

become evident as this saga unfolds,

Purifying the bloodline of Agape that

links us eternally, soul to soul

One could misconstrue the deep lump in

their throat as a sign that something's

wrong, but the butterflies in the pit of

your stomach are motivated by something

entirely too strong

Thine course is aligned and set in motion

as are the stars,

Yet sometimes fear of things unknown
prevents us from realizing just who we
are
Half circles of energy held captive in a
world with no walls, holding back while
searching for matching halves we
frequently stumble and sometimes fall,
Sometimes no words are the best words
of all,
And sometimes we are so high on emotions;
we don't notice the pain when we fall.

What Used To Be

Previously seen the temporary thing

that was once you and me

I didn't know what to call US when we

were one

And I still can't describe what IT was

now that we're done

But mixed feelings linger about you, me

and the in-between

Of what I've seen to be very promising

things

Reduced to yet another bittersweet

memory of what used to be

The wonderful conversations and

profound letters that used to be

The "Hey Baby" you'd hear from me

And the genuine smile that used to be

exclusively, for me

The intensity between the sheets before

we drifted to sleep

And the awakening of us that used to be

The beauty of what used to be is

replaced by analytical thoughts

About the parts of me you say 'conflict

with where you want to be spiritually'

Followed by thoughts of "the place" you

are now that is seemingly beyond me

And apparently the cause of this empty

space that used to be filled with you and

me

Things perceived of what used to be

certainly vary between you and me

Because what you said was a hindrance to
you was actually a blessing for me
They say hindsight is 20/20 and looking
back it's quite clear to me that
The friends we were beginning to be is
what I'm really missing
About the you and me that used to be

My Wealth

The wealth I have to give is my

experience

packaged in the wisdom of knowing

Showing my worth in the consistency of

the results I produce

when I put in work to improve the

impression of footprints that the future

may follow

When KG quipped poetically I was

inclined to agree,

"I am who I am and who I'm not I'll

never be"

so my richness lies in the authenticity of

me being me

An uncanny ability to exercise humility

while watering seeds in the discomfort

of my own flaws

I wash away the residue of outmoded

thinking as

Words of hydration spill in fields of

edification to yield

rewards buried beneath the fertile soil

of my mind

My wealth is easy to see but difficult to

find

when you search for it with abusive intent

amplified by bad vibes

My resources will not be squandered by

the selfish habits of those that live in a

cul de sac of dead ends littered with

false friendships

Cause the ones I'm rockin wit

Pour into me

Look into me and see beauty beyond the

tragedy of trauma

One way streets of friendships don't do

shit for me so I make U turns and bend

the block

Till I find a spot to park and ball out

wit a team that bounces prosperity like

playing roundball is a metaphor for their

reality

Cause they see the divining line between

what's real and what could be

If there was LASIK for our souls when

we struggle to see how far dreams can

go

it would be in the circle that forms from

the alchemy of progress

that we dress ourselves in

We don uniforms of persistence that have

been custom fitted to discover more of

ourselves

To shake off the programming that

wants to make us carbon copies of someone

else

Building another dreamer's wealth at the

expense of our own health while arguing

the nobility of sacrifices for the ones we

love begs the question

Are you willing to grind day and night

for your own aspirations when you realize

the value of return on investment?

The Upside

The pressure of this existence

can be a harrowing experience for all

that have been enlisted

But even more so for those committed to

live this finite life

takin strides to do more than just get by

There is an upside

See

Those are the types

that receive the weight of this pressure

multiplied by the purpose they've been

commissioned to represent

while the world bear's witness

It hits different

because eyes have a unique design

that can transmogrify the scope of what
they scrutinize
When measuring the efforts of others
against the triggers they hold inside
The insecurities that reside behind the
filter of self-conceit

Become a double-edged sword that
scores the target it abhors with
sabotage and deceit
Errant tongues swing words like weapons
with malicious intent
While claiming self-defense because even
villains get blindsided by the
righteousness of their own convictions
On a deeper level we're all innocent
victims of ignorance

But the pressure can be so intense

We lose sight of the guidance the

universe keeps giving

as it hopes we learn to dismiss all the

distractions long enough to listen

to the repetitive whisper written on the

wind meant to replenish our souls

As the galaxy tries to remind us that we

are

the evolution the divine chose

And if we can get our focus to let the

pressure

go

We might find ourselves wading in the

sweet

spot

where consistency meets growth

Emergence

I was incubated in living water but the
geography of my birth made me a
candidate for a classism driven
slaughter
And each day offers an opportunity to
survive the vastness of these troubled
waters
Every time I wake up and take up the
mantle of my ancestral line
I am fighting to survive a society
designed
for every demographic but mine
All the while preserving the black gold
that
holds forever within my DNA chain

The wards of 14/88 framed the beauty

of my

melanated existence with poisonous liquids

leaving a bad taste in my mouth

And the flavor gets a bit more prominent

when sipping tea in the Deep South

If church is wherever two or more are

gathered

Why does the baptism of this world

reality feel like a competition to see how

long I can live

without the ability to breathe

Bad intentions try forcing me to drink

deep

ignoring air bubbles of protest to this

travesty

I'm trying to escape

as a hand hostile to hope holds my voice

hostage beneath tumultuous waters

Maybe the design of this prescribed

demise was promoted to see if the magic

the divine gifted me carries the

combination code our souls seek for

liberation

While they compromise what you see with

your eyes

Blurred truth is hard to identify

But the animosity behind hidden hands

seeking my premature demise is still

thick in the air

And that invisible grip is still strong
enough to mitigate slips despite the slow
drip of struggle
Because the goal is make me believe the
elite control the atmosphere of my
existence
The hands that make this world go round
really don't care because they holding
the trump cards and there isn't enough
of us fed up enough to jump froggy on a
dare

But I know my truth so peep the scene
and maybe you'll see that lies are the
only thing dying there

My roots run deep because I am the

tree of life others seek to pluck fruit

from

I was born beautiful before children of

corruption came to get some

And my melanin enriches the soil

surrounding my roots

the skin of my produce protects the

fruit of truth meant for nourishment in

this world

My coriolis effect directs the flow

controls the dose distributed to

unsaturated seeds

With raised hands and muted voices that

sing a soliloquy

About starving for the wisdom that falls
from my trees
My vitality is the subtle desire in a room
of thieves with eyes that scream pick me
I know I'm good so you don't have to root
for me
Because the fog blocking your vision
prevents access to the depths your lost
soul needs to see
My body begins below but as I break
silence wit my complex simplicity
A balance of energy sprouts beauty that
adds more than color to circumstance
Drink deep from my wellspring and
consume the orange zest of my
sustenance

I'm tempted to ask you not to assume

the image of me be askew

because apples hid the lie that turned

the first

man into a fool

And I'm here to lead the escape from

the prison of ignorance you thought you

found

freedom in

Never took a deep a breath but your soul

is

yearning to breathe again

You heard about the sun but the shade

got you too comfortable to get heated

And shade may be cool to you but

if I'm the tree and Vitamin D is a need

then take a direct hit of the rays that

raised me

Revitalize those deficiencies

Because it's a tragedy to me

That my green is the stuff of

unnecessary envy as my purpose is to

feed anyone open enough

to receive

I am creation submerged meant to

emerge

from the persistent shine of healing

light

But your mind gotta be open

before you can set your frequency to the

vibrations in this circle of life

I went looking for healing

And planted roots in clouds of peace

Embracing serenity cultivated in the

fertility

of discomfort because the richness of

the soil

I chose came wit a money back guarantee

Allowing me to bask in an existence free

of the malice that tried to smother the

best parts of me

For All I Know

Life's temperament can be hot or cold

sometimes it unfolds like a cruel joke

For all I know

My soul is a conduit for wisdom

In the Dewey decimal system

I'm listed as essential for edification on
this plane of existence

And my pen is the medium enlisted to
make sense of it

The timbre of my voice was the galaxies
choice for motivated listening

But I might be trippin on the shoelaces
of my own ego

A pitfall for the ignorantly
educated with corrugated goals

Dying to live while trying to give
relevant gifts to my circle of friends
like every day is Christmas

and I'm trying to unwrap the truth of
it

Sometimes I tie randomly gathered
strings of knowledge together for the
masses that need direction

So I don't forget that my shoes fit
these life events I've been tasked to
take action in

 Maybe my perspective is meant as a tool
for rehearsing the verse

you plan to lay across beats made by the
universe

My analytical mind moves in 6/4 time

it's complicated nature is a gift and a
curse balanced by a practiced flow

Controlled chaos by a moon child mixing a
natural style that is inherently wild

with the consistency of routine

For all I know this scene was set for
me to fertilize prompts with seeds

incubated at ninety-eight degrees
watered soulfully

 I guess I'll find out

if what I serve deserves consumption

If ever I'm engaged when no longer on
stage

after I put my pen away for a brief
vacay

From fighting the solitary confinement
of self-deprecating thoughts looking for
a place to stay

Forgiveness

Hey you
Yeah,
you with face
Come here
I got something to say
But wait
I know it's hard to see me through the
toothpaste
You forgot to wipe away
Mirror stained
as you rushed to start your day
But it's ok

You got a lot on your plate
and sometimes you worry about what
others consume
Instead of staying in tune with what you
ate

Woah!
easy now big fella
No need to poke your chest out
This ain't that and that ain't what this is
about
I don't want no problem wit you
As a matter of fact I got a gift for you
Call it an intervention since you're in a
mood
And it's cool
I sensed it and I'm not gonna dismiss it
Because I cut for you

Ohhhh
You too
Bet
I think it's safe to say
We're making our way to the same line on
the same page
And I booked this fight
I mean flight

Three

Six

Twelve

Because your distress beacon is blinking

and it's clear we need help

I just wanna say

I forgive you

I see the way you looking at we

I'm saying you

but I mean me

Listen

Let's not complicate this thing

Look

my hands

are up

I come in peace

Because now I see the fullness of you

And I want you

No

I need you to forgive me
For investing my attention and energy
into so many things
That kept us from becoming
the best we
can be

When I say you while looking at me
What I mean is
I'm all for
Giving we a reprieve from self
sabotaging thoughts that left me
tormented
And even though I meant it when I
initially made the commitment
My heart was there but the discipline
was missing

Causing a promising dream to devolve into
misery

I've seen men become torn as they tried
to forge a path of success on the road of
fallacy
I know those routes like the back of my
hand you see
And I forgive me
for every hill I built and tried to climb
only to fall back into a saddle of
depression
I forgive me for falling off ridges into
a valley of bruises and contusions made of
unlearned lessons

Only to start building a new road to more
dams instead of seeking relief
I forgive me for ignoring these finely
contoured
lines that defined
The depth of this ever changing
landscape of fate
From unwise decisions I made

I forgive me because I had a revelation
That my greatness is still chomping at
the bit
And now that I
Wait
I mean now that we are doing the healing
thing
of forgiving me
We moving into a season of winning

As a prophet that profits when
Progress
Is
My
Process
And the wait is less because of the
weight we
left on the table as we tapped in
To access the physician within ourselves

Because now I'm all in for healing
thyself